COOL

Metal

PROJECTS

Creative Ways to Upcycle Your Trash into Treasure

A Division of ABDO

ABDO
Publishing Company

PAM SCHEUNEMANN

visit us at www.abdopublishing.com

Published by ABDO Publishing Company, a division of ABDO,
P.O. Box 398166, Minneapolis, Minnesota 55439. Copyright
© 2013 by Abdo Consulting Group, Inc. International
copyrights reserved in all countries. No part of this book may
be reproduced in any form without written permission from
the publisher. Checkerboard Library™ is a trademark and
logo of ABDO Publishing Company.

Printed in the United States of America, North Mankato,
Minnesota
062012
092012

DESIGN AND PRODUCTION: ANDERS HANSON, MIGHTY MEDIA, INC.
SERIES EDITOR: LIZ SALZMANN
PHOTO CREDITS: SHUTTERSTOCK

The following manufacturers/names appearing in this book
are trademarks: Fiskars®, Glitter Glue™, Goo Gone®, Mod
Podge®, Painter's Mate Green®, Rust-oleum®, Sharpie®

LIBRARY OF CONGRESS CATALOGING-IN-PUBLICATION DATA

Scheunemann, Pam, 1955-
  Cool metal projects : creative ways to upcycle your trash
into treasure / Pam Scheunemann.
      p. cm. -- (Cool trash to treasure)
  Includes index.
  ISBN 978-1-61783-434-9
  1. Scrap metals--Recycling--Juvenile literature. 2. Metal-
work--Juvenile literature. I. Title.
  TT214.S34 2012
  745.56--dc23
                              2011052615

TABLE of CONTENTS

Trash to Treasure   4

A Fresh Look at Metal   6

Tools & Materials   8

Get the Message   10

Tin Can Organizer   14

License to Write   18

Glittery Box   20

Can Tab Earrings   24

Earring Grill   28

Conclusion   30

Glossary   31

Web Sites   31

Index   32

TRASH TO Treasure

THE SKY'S THE LIMIT

The days of throwing everything in the trash are long over. Recycling has become a part of everyday life. To recycle means to use something again or to find a new use for it. By creating treasures out of trash, we are also *upcycling*. This is a term used to **describe** making useful items out of things that may have been put in the trash.

Maybe you've been putting all your cans in the recycling bin. Why not take a fresh look at all those cans and give them new life? They are easily **available**. Everyone's got a few empty cans lying around. See what you can come up with. The sky's the limit.

Permission and Safety

- Always get **permission** before making any type of craft at home.
- Ask if you can use the tools and materials needed.
- Ask for help when you need it.
- Be careful when using knives, scissors, or other sharp objects.
- Be especially careful when working with cans, the edges can be very sharp!

Be Prepared

- Read the entire activity before you begin.
- Make sure you have all the tools and materials listed.
- Keep your work area clean and organized.
- Follow the directions carefully.
- Clean up after you are finished for the day.

Most metal other than cans cannot be recycled. These include things such as metal trays, baskets, and **hardware**. It is even more important to look for ways to upcycle these items.

In this book you'll find great ideas to upcycle different kinds of metal. Make them just like they appear here or use your own ideas. You can make them for yourself or as gifts for others. These projects use easy-to-find tools and materials.

METAL

Many everyday items are made of metal. Metal can be found all around us. It's in cans, license plates, cookie tins, and more. Here are some ideas for reusing or upcycling metal.

Aluminum Cans

Cans come in many sizes. Here are some things they can be made into.

- VASES
- PENCIL HOLDERS
- STORAGE CONTAINERS
- CANDLE HOLDERS

GET THE MESSAGE

Make your own chalkboard!

1. Sand any rust off the surface of the tray.

2. Wash the sanding dust off and dry the tray thoroughly.

3. Put painter's tape around the edge of the tray. Cut slits in the tape to bend it around the corners. Be sure to line up the bottom edges so you have a smooth painting line.

4. If possible, do this step outside. Cover your work area with newspaper. Paint the tray with rusty metal primer. Follow the directions on the paint can. Let the primer dry completely. Add more coats if needed.

Continued on the next page

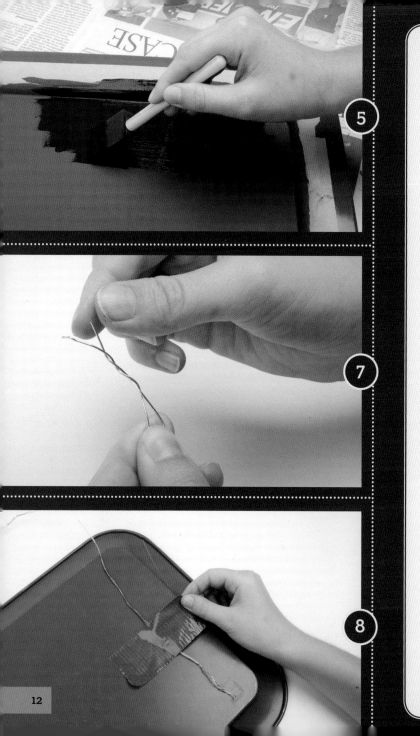

5   Apply the chalkboard paint evenly. Follow the directions on the can. Add more coats if needed. Let it dry completely after each coat.

6   Carefully remove the painter's tape.

7   Cut a piece of wire four times longer than the width of the tray. Fold it in half and twist together.

8   Lay one end along one side of the back of the tray. Put a piece of duct tape over the wire. Leave about 4 inches (10 cm) of wire below the tape.

9 Fold the extra wire up over the duct tape. Wrap it tightly around the wire above the duct tape.

10 Repeat steps 8 and 9 to tape the other end of the wire to the other side of the tray.

11 Pull the wire toward the center of the top of the tray. That is the point the tray will hang from. Put a piece of duct tape over the wire about an inch (3 cm) below the the hanging point. This will keep the tray from tilting away from the wall.

12 Decorate the border of the tray. Use glitter glue, gems, or whatever you like.

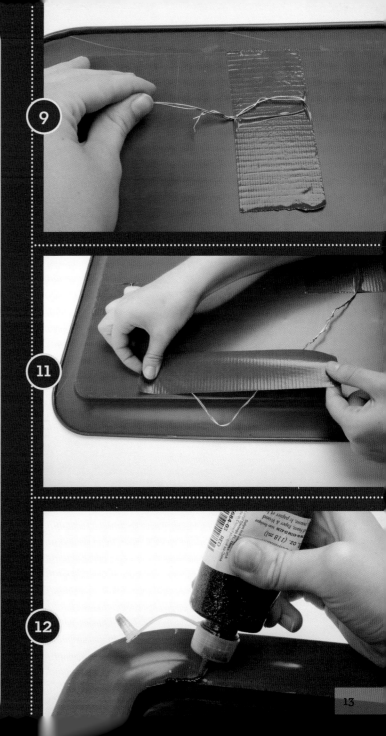

STUFF YOU'LL NEED

- 7 OR MORE TIN CANS (SAME SIZE)
- CARDBOARD
- MARKER
- SCISSORS
- CRAFT FELT
- RULER
- GLUE
- WOODEN SKEWER
- HOT GLUE AND GLUE GUN
- PICTURE HANGERS

TIN CAN ORGANIZER

This storage is totally tubular!

1   Wash the cans thoroughly. Let them dry.

2   Wrap the felt around the can. Cut it so the sides just meet.

3   Measure the height of the can. Mark the height on the felt in two places. Draw a line between the marks and cut along the line. Cut more felt rectangles this size. You will need two rectangles for each can. They can be the same color or different colors.

4   Set a can on a piece of cardboard. Trace around the can with a marker. Cut out the circle inside the lines. Make sure the circle fits in the bottom of the can. Cut it smaller if necessary.

Continued on the next page

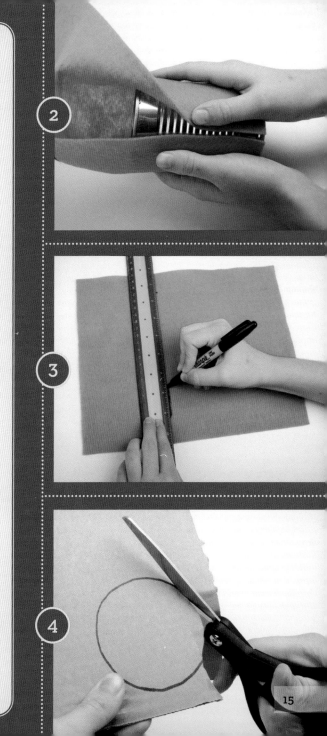

5 Trace around the cardboard circle on a piece of felt. Cut it out. Make sure it fits in the can. Glue it inside the bottom of a can.

6 Put one of the felt rectangles around the inside of the can. If the sides **overlap**, trim it until they meet.

7 Put the felt back in the can. Fold the sides back. Use a wooden skewer to put glue along the seam. Press the sides against the inside of the can.

8 Put glue around the top edges of the can. Press the felt against the can. Smooth out any wrinkles with the clean end of the wooden skewer.

9 Put glue around the edges and in the middle of another felt rectangle.

10 Wrap the felt around the outside of the can. Press the seam together. Add a bit more glue along the seam.

11 Repeat steps 5 through 10 with the other cans. Let the glue dry overnight.

12 Arrange the cans the way you want the organizer to look.

13 Have an adult help you use the hot glue gun. Glue the cans together. Put the glue along the seams in the felt. That way the seams won't show. Be sure to put glue everywhere the cans touch each other.

14 Use hot glue to glue a picture hanger to the bottom of one or two cans. Store your stuff with style!

- **2 OLD LICENSE PLATES**
- **MARKER**
- **CRAFT FELT**
- **SCISSORS**
- **HOLE PUNCH**
- **DOUBLE-SIDED TAPE**
- **TAG BOARD**
- **PAPER**
- **2 LOOSE-LEAF BOOK RINGS**

LICENSE TO WRITE

Car not included!

1. Wash and dry the license plates. Set a license plate on the felt. Trace around it with a marker. Make dots where the top two holes are. Cut out the felt just inside the marker line. Punch out the holes. Cut a second piece of felt the same way.

2. Put double-sided tape all around the edges of the back of both license plates. Put some in the middle too. Stick a piece of felt to each license plate.

3. Cut a piece of tag board a little smaller than the license plates. Cut a second piece of tag board and a bunch of paper the same size.

4. Put one of the tag board rectangles under a license plate. Make it even with the top edge. Center it between the sides of the license plate. Make marks where the holes are. Punch the holes out of the tag board.

5. Use the tag board as a **template** to punch holes in the same places on the other tag board rectangle and the sheets of paper.

6. Put the paper between the tag board rectangles. Put a license plate on each side. Put a book ring through each hole.

19

STUFF YOU'LL NEED

- OLD TIN BOX
- PAINTER'S TAPE
- NEWSPAPER
- SPARKLE MOD PODGE
- SMALL PAINTBRUSH
- GLITTER
- CRAFT KNIFE (OPTIONAL)
- FOAM BRUSH

GLITTERY BOX

Storage space in a cool case!

1. Take the lid off the box. Use painter's tape to cover the top edge of the box where the lid sits. There shouldn't be any glitter there.

2. You will apply the glitter one color at a time. Put tape around the areas where you want to put the first color of glitter. Smooth the edges with your fingernail so they are tight against the box.

3. Put tape over the rim of the lid. Then tape around the areas on the lid where you want to put the first color of glitter.

Continued on the next page

4 Spread newspaper over your work area. Use a small paintbrush to put Sparkle Mod Podge inside the taped areas on the box. Sprinkle the first color of glitter over the Mod Podge. Make sure the area is covered completely. Gently tap the box to knock off the extra glitter. If you missed any spots, just add a little more Mod Podge and glitter. Tap off the extra.

5 Repeat step 4 on the lid. Brush the exposed areas of the lid with Mod Podge. Add glitter and gently tap off the extra. Let both pieces dry completely. Pour the extra glitter from the newspaper back into its container.

6 Once the Mod Podge is completely dry, carefully remove the tape. You may want to use a craft knife to cut along the edge of the tape for a smooth line. Leave the tape on the edge of the box and lid.

7. Tape off the areas for the second color. You don't need to put tape over the first color of glitter. The glitter forms a border for the second color. Brush on the Mod Podge. Be careful not to put any on the dry glitter. Add the second color of glitter and tap off the extra. Let it dry completely.

8. Repeat steps 6 and 7 until the box and lid are covered with glitter. Let it dry completely.

9. Remove the tape from the edges of the box and lid. Use a foam brush to cover the box and lid with one or two coats of Sparkle Mod Podge. Let it dry completely after each coat.

STUFF YOU'LL NEED

- SODA CAN TABS
- FLAT-NOSED PLIERS
- COLORED WIRE (22 GAUGE)
- WIRE CUTTERS
- RULER
- FLAT-NOSED PLIERS
- HEAD PINS
- SMALL BEADS
- EAR WIRES
- COLORED JUMP RINGS

CAN TAB EARRINGS

Mix and match!

1. If any of the tabs still have the flap where it was attached to the can, use a flat-nosed pliers to remove it.

2. Cut two pieces of colored wire about 3 inches (8 cm) long.

3. Wrap both wires around the thinner loop on a tab. Put one wire on each side of the loop.

4. There will be a gap between the wires. Use a flat-nosed pliers to press the ends down so they don't stick out.

Continued on the next page

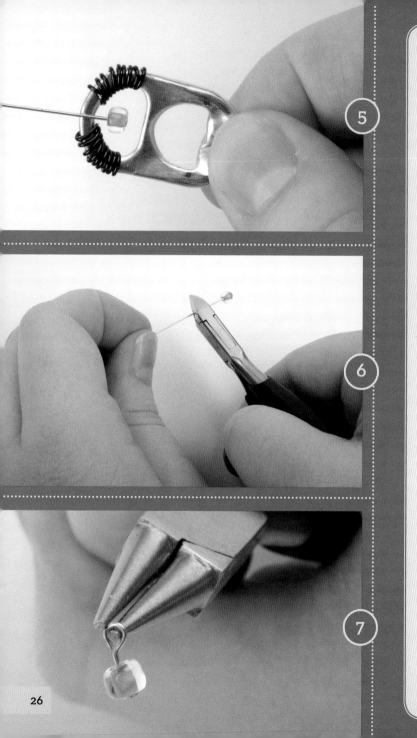

5. Put a small bead on a head pin. Make sure the bead fits inside the loop you wrapped the wires around.

6. Use the wire cutters to trim the head pin wire. Cut it about ¼ inch (.6 cm) from the bead.

7. Use the round-nosed pliers to make a loop in the head pin wire above the bead. Bend the wire to one side. Then grab the end of the wire with the pliers and twist to form a loop. Use the pliers to close the gap if needed.

8. Use the pliers to twist open the end of an ear wire. Hang the bead on the ear wire by the loop you made.

9. Put the ear wire loop around the can tab between the colored wire. Close the loop on the ear wire with the pliers.

10. Use the pliers to gently open the colored jump rings. Hold one side and use the pliers to twist one end to the side. Do not pull the ends away from each other. Put the rings on the other loop of the can tab. Close the rings.

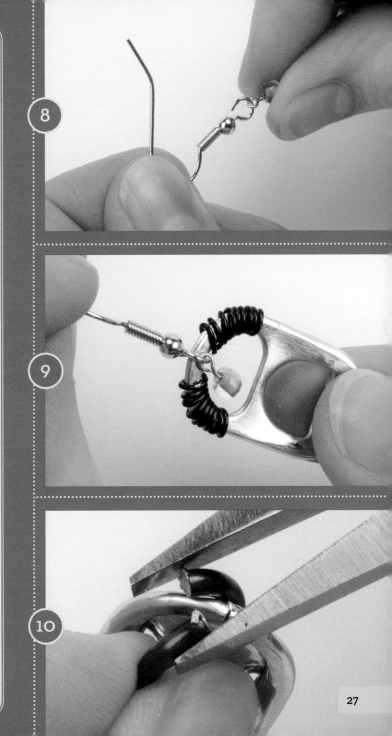

27

Earring Grill

1. Cut a piece of ribbon about 36 inches (91 cm) long. Use the glue stick to put some glue on the end. Wrap the ribbon around the edges of the **grill**. Secure the end with glue. Cut more ribbon and repeat until the entire edge is covered.

2. Have an adult help you use the hot glue gun. Glue the beads to the back of the grill. Spread them out evenly around the rim. Place the beads with the holes pointing out to the side. Let the glue dry.

3. Cut four pieces of ribbon about 18 inches (46 cm) long. Unfold a paper clip and use it to push a ribbon through each bead. Bring the ends of each ribbon around the rim and tie them into bows.

4. Cut another ribbon about 36 inches (91 cm) long. Fold it in half. Put the ends between the top two grill wires from back to front. One end should be on each side of the center wire. Hold the middle of the ribbon above the rim of the grill. Bring the ends of the ribbon over the rim and through the loop made by the middle of the ribbon. Pull it tight. Tie the ends together. Hang up the grill and add your earrings!

CONCLUSION

Now you know what upcycling is all about. What hidden gems do you have around your house? Do you have relatives who need their **attic** cleaned? What about **garage** and yard sales? Are there **thrift stores** and reuse centers near you? These are all great sources for materials that you can upcycle!

There are many benefits to upcycling. You can make some really great stuff for yourself or gifts for your family and friends. You can save useful things from going into the trash. And the best part is, you don't have to spend a lot of money doing it!

So keep your eyes and ears open for new ideas. There are many Web sites that are all about recycling and upcycling. You might find ideas on TV or in magazines. There are endless ways that you can make something beautiful and useful from **discarded** materials. Remember, the sky's the limit!

GLOSSARY

ATTIC – a room right under the roof of a building.

AVAILABLE – able to be had or used.

DESCRIBE – to tell about something with words or pictures.

DISCARD – to throw away.

GARAGE – a room or building that cars are kept in. A *garage sale* is a sale that takes place in a garage.

GRILL – a device with parallel metal bars on which food is cooked.

HARDWARE – metal tools and supplies used to build things.

OVERLAP – to lie partly on top of something.

PERMISSION – when a person in charge says it's okay to do something.

TEMPLATE – a shape you draw or cut around to copy it onto something else.

THRIFT STORE – a store that sells used items, especially one that is run by a charity.

Web sites

To learn more about cool craft projects, visit ABDO Publishing Company on the World Wide Web at www.abdopublishing.com. Web sites about creative ways for upcycling trash are featured on our Book Links page. These links are routinely monitored and updated to provide the most current information available.

INDEX

C

Chalkboard, project for, 10-13

D

Decorative box, project for, 20-23

Directions, reading and following, 5

E

Earring organizer, project for, 28-29

Earrings, project for, 24-27

G

Gifts, making, 5, 30

J

Journal, project for, 18-19

M

Metal

cleaning, 7

projects using, 4, 6, 7, 10-13, 14-17, 18-19, 20-23, 24-27, 28-29

sources of, 4-5, 6-7

O

Organizer, project for, 14-17

P

Permission, to do projects, 5

Preparing, to do projects, 5

R

Recycling, 4-5

S

Safety guidelines, for projects, 5

Sharp objects, safe use of, 5

Storage container, project for, 14-17

T

Tools and materials

cleaning, 7

list of, 8-9

organizing, 5

permission to use, 5

sources of, 4-5, 6-7, 30

U

Upcycling

benefits of, 30

definition of, 4

projects for, 4-5, 30, 31

W

Web sites, about craft projects, 30, 31

Work area, organizing and cleaning, 5